MY THOUGHTS

VOLUME - I

PRADIP MOLSOM

Preface

This book contains my thoughts, written from my imaginations, observations, and experiences.

1.
We exist. Our minds live.

- Pradip Molsom

2.

When we close our eyes, we can see the entire universe.

- Pradip Molsom

3.

Life is mysterious and limited, as we all know, but its limitations give us a hint that there is something beyond life.

- Pradip Molsom

4.

Everything makes sense if our minds are not too limited.

- Pradip Molsom

5.

We are not alone; we have our mind with us.

- *Pradip Molsom*

6.

When you realize you are an energy in your body, you begin to see things in a new light.

- Pradip Molsom

7.

Everyone has the ability to learn, but only a few have the ability to reason.

- Pradip Molsom

8.
Do we really know something when we think we know it?

- Pradip Molsom

9.

To know something is to know nothing at all.

- Pradip Molsom

10.
Were those "new ideas" or "thoughts" truly new, or were they merely reminiscences of the past?

- Pradip Molsom

11.

We live in the same society, but our mental worlds are different from one another.

- *Pradip Molsom*

12.

The majority will be imprisoned in their ignorant reality, and only a select few will be able to break free it.

- Pradip Molsom

13.

When the authenticity is laid bare, no one is captivated, but when an illusionary narrative is unfolded, everyone is rashly enthralled.

- Pradip Molsom

14.

To discover something new, we must set out on our own.

- Pradip Molsom

15.

Only seeing and not showing is selfishness. Only showing without seeing is stupidity.

- Pradip Molsom

16.

The more our inner power grows, the more humble we become.

- Pradip Molsom

17.

When we hate others, we are actually hating ourselves because we are all wired up at the center.

- *Pradip Molsom*

18.

Imitating other people's ideas prevents us from being true to ourselves. So, rather than imitating, let us be unique and creative in our thinking.

- Pradip Molsom

19.

When we love with our minds, we are actually calculative, which means our love is fake; when we love with our hearts, our love is real.

- Pradip Molsom

20.

Life goes on as it always has, is, and will go on.

- Pradip Molsom

21.

Everything is connected, yet it is difficult to connect.

- Pradip Molsom

22.

Our physical eyes have a limited range of vision, but our minds can see far beyond what our physical eyes can.

- Pradip Molsom

23.

Our inner world, like the universe, is infinite.

- Pradip Molsom

24.
True knowledge lies within us, not externally.

- Pradip Molsom

25.

When you realize you have devolved into nothing, you have actually started to understand yourself.

- *Pradip Molsom*

26.

The only thing I am capable of is being nothing.

- Pradip Molsom

27.
I am nothing because I know nothing.

- Pradip Molsom

28.

If you cannot empty your mind, you will not be able to generate something novel from within. However, emptying one's mind is perhaps the most difficult task.

- *Pradip Molsom*

29.

When your mind is active, your mouth will be inactive.

- Pradip Molsom

30.

When the mind is inactive, it is as good as dead.

- Pradip Molsom

31.

Rather than being proud of my accomplishments, I am ashamed of my ignorance.

- *Pradip Molsom*

32.

It is impossible for a man to learn who thinks he already knows the things.

- Pradip Molsom

33.

It is sad to say, but it is true: there are some people who showcase love outwardly while boiling inwardly.

- Pradip Molsom

34.

Before you say something hurtful to someone else, take a look at yourself.

- Pradip Molsom

35.

If you treat everyone with love, you will be the happiest person.

- Pradip Molsom

36.

Dependence makes you incompetent.

- Pradip Molsom

37.

I chose to become nothing because it frees me from all influences.

- Pradip Molsom

38.

Be the type of person who solves problems rather than creating them.

- Pradip Molsom

39.

When you do something, do not expect anything in return. Just keep doing what you are doing.

- *Pradip Molsom*

40.

Do not let problems control you. You will not be able to stand if you keep all of your problems inside you.

- Pradip Molsom

41.

Never trust those whose emotions change over time; instead, trust those whose emotions remain consistent over time.

- Pradip Molsom

42.
Overthinking is a disease that leads to suffering.

- *Pradip Molsom*

43.

We are small, but our world is vast. Our world is small, but the universe is vast.

- Pradip Molsom

44.

When you interact with your mind, you are communicating with the universe.

- Pradip Molsom

45.

We have rejected the truth and replaced it with lies.

- Pradip Molsom

46.

I wonder why we are so obsessed with becoming like others when we could instead become like ourselves, which is totally unique.

- Pradip Molsom

47.
Most of us are trapped in negative thoughts, which is why we have issues, worries, hatred, feelings of inadequacy and so on.

- *Pradip Molsom*

48.

Certain things, despite their existence, cannot be explained with words. We have to accept them as they are.

- Pradip Molsom

49.

Keep an eye on what is going around you or you will be duped.

- Pradip Molsom

50.

Since our universe is an open space, I believe that nothing can be hidden.

- Pradip Molsom

51.

If your heart is weak, work on strengthening it so that you do not suffer unnecessarily.

- Pradip Molsom

52.

Do we truly know one another?
Because I am not who you think I am,
and you are not who I think you are.
Only you can know about true yourself,
not anyone else.

- *Pradip Molsom*

53.

We are only here for a short time, so why not live without hatred, ego, judging, and comparison, but with love?

- Pradip Molsom

54.

We seek God in churches and other religious institutions, but do we give God a place within us, in our hearts? How can we find God if we do not make room for Him in our hearts? I believe that God cannot be found outside; God is within us, in our hearts. So, in order to stay truly connected to God, we must first build the church of God in our hearts.

- Pradip Molsom

55.
We began by learning "how to live?"
Finally, we figured out "how to leave?

- Pradip Molsom

56.

I am very limited in terms of material possessions and knowledge, but my imagination knows no bounds.

- Pradip Molsom

57.

If you want to be wise, you must remain a fool in the eyes of others.

- *Pradip Molsom*

58.

Life cannot be measured or discovered by the mind because it has no beginning or end.

- Pradip Molsom

59.

When we see with open eyes, we see only a limited number of possibilities, but when we close our eyes, we see an infinite number of possibilities.

- Pradip Molsom

60.

It is lovable and yet hard to love.

- Pradip Molsom

61.

I frequently failed to hold my thoughts because they only came to visit me for a fraction of a second.

- Pradip Molsom

62.

The thing is when I think I can't think.

- Pradip Molsom

63.

Be a fan of yourself.

- Pradip Molsom

64.
Be a dreamer, not a specialist in any field of knowledge.

- Pradip Molsom

65.
If you cannot control your tongue, you will lose your value.

- Pradip Molsom

66.

Do not hide your attitude. Show your true attitude because that is who you really are.

- Pradip Molsom

67.

Great minds are those who can think beyond the confines of a syllabus or a book.

- Pradip Molsom

68.

Do not let your past hold you captive; it cannot be changed, so you must accept it as it is. However, the present and the future are entirely under your control.

- Pradip Molsom

69.

I am a curious person who is not a specialist in any field. I spent the most of my time observing, listening, thinking, learning, and expressing myself verbally or in writing.

- Pradip Molsom

70.

You may be enormous, but if your mind is small, you will struggle to move ahead.

- *Pradip Molsom*

71.

Do not get caught up in the field of physical time; instead, be a timeless person.

- Pradip Molsom

72.

For many, there is a distinction between day and night, but for a few, there is none.

- Pradip Molsom

73.

If you do not believe in yourself, how can you have faith in God? Believing in yourself is the same thing as having faith in God.

- Pradip Molsom

74.

If we cannot even understand what this is all about, how can we possibly understand ourselves?

- Pradip Molsom

75.

Only an eccentric can understand another eccentric's thoughts.

- Pradip Molsom

76.

When you are weak, you only have yourself to rely on.

- Pradip Molsom

77.

The earth does not belong just to you or me; it is our collective home. Maps are merely political views rather than factual evidence.

- Pradip Molsom

78.

Take a deep dive within yourself. You will discover and learn something entirely new and meaningful.

- Pradip Molsom

79.

Keep your mind open and free, and listen carefully; you will hear the voice of God.

- Pradip Molsom

80.

I can see but I find hard to see.

- *Pradip Molsom*

81.

Assess yourself carefully; there are many resources within you that have yet to be unearthed.

- *Pradip Molsom*

82.

When I look at things with my physical eyes, I see nothing, but when I look at things with my mental eyes, I see everything.

- Pradip Molsom

83.

I am just a body, and you are my breath of life.

- Pradip Molsom

84.
The only thing we truly need in life is peace.

- Pradip Molsom

85.

When you believe something exists, it certainly does, which is why you could perceive it.

- Pradip Molsom

86.

I believe that we can only rethink things that already exist in our universe.

- Pradip Molsom

87.

I don't know what I don't know. When I realised what I did not know, I realised I had not learned anything.

- *Pradip Molsom*

88.

Thoughts do not come when you are prepared; rather, they come when your mind is completely free and unaware.

- Pradip Molsom

89.

To be happy in life, I believe that one should not hate, have less expectations, avoid negativity, remain calm, and stay connected to God.

- *Pradip Molsom*

90.

Sad to say, most of us are only physically alive and mentally dead.

- Pradip Molsom

91.

If you can imagine, you can definitely accomplish. So, if your mind can reach, you can reach physically.

- Pradip Molsom

92.

When I make a promise to you, it is not just a promise from me. It is a divine promise.

- Pradip Molsom

93.

Nothing is the beginning, and nothing is the end.

- Pradip Molsom

94.
Mindless truth is totally pointless.

- Pradip Molsom

95.

There is neither life nor love without the other.

- Pradip Molsom

96.

I was not aware of my ignorance before, but at least now I am.

- Pradip Molsom

97.
A well-educated person has a free mind.

- Pradip Molsom

98.

Sometime life will hit you so hard that you feel like you are going to lose your way, but stay strong and do not give up. Life is never easy and never straightforward.

- Pradip Molsom

99.

Between life and death, there is living.
So, live each day to the fullest.

- Pradip Molsom

100.

Truth is not easily obtained. Truth cannot be found by seeking it; rather, it finds us when we are not seeking it.

- Pradip Molsom

101.

Outer beauty will only bring you temporary happiness, but inner beauty will bring you eternal happiness.

- Pradip Molsom

102.

Leave a mark before you leave.

- Pradip Molsom

Printed by Libri Plureos GmbH in Hamburg,
Germany